THE BOOK OF Luke

ONE CHAPTER A DAY

GoodMorningGirls.org

The Book of Luke

© 2017 Women Living Well Ministries, LLC

ALL RIGHTS RESERVED

No part of this book may be reproduced in any form or by any electronic or mechanical means, including information storage and retrieval systems, without written permission from the author, except in the case of a reviewer, who may quote brief passages embodied in critical articles or in a review.

Scripture is from the ESV® Bible (The Holy Bible, English Standard Version®), copyright © 2001 by Crossway Bibles, a publishing ministry of Good News Publishers. Used by permission. All rights reserved.

Welcome to Good Morning Girls! We are so glad you are joining us.

God created us to walk with Him, to know Him, and to be loved by Him. He is our living well, and when we drink from the water He continually provides, His living water will change the entire course of our lives.

> *Jesus said: "Whoever drinks of the water that I will give him will never be thirsty again. The water that I will give him will become in him a spring of water welling up to eternal life." ~ John 4:14 (ESV)*

So let's begin.

The method we use here at GMG is called the **SOAK** method.

- ❒ **S**—The S stands for *Scripture*—Read the chapter for the day. Then choose 1-2 verses and write them out word for word. (There is no right or wrong choice—just let the Holy Spirit guide you.)

- ❒ **O**—The O stands for *Observation*—Look at the verse or verses you wrote out. Write 1 or 2 observations. What stands out to you? What do you learn about the character of God from these verses? Is there a promise, command or teaching?

- ❒ **A**—The A stands for *Application*—Personalize the verses. What is God saying to you? How can you apply them to your life? Are there any changes you need to make or an action to take?

- ❒ **K**—The K stands for *Kneeling in Prayer*—Pause, kneel and pray. Confess any sin God has revealed to you today. Praise God for His word. Pray the passage over your own life or someone you love. Ask God to help you live out your applications.

SOAK God's word into your heart and squeeze every bit of nourishment you can out of each day's scripture reading. Soon you will find your life transformed by the renewing of your mind!

Walk with the King!

Courtney

WomenLivingWell.org, GoodMorningGirls.org

Join the GMG Community

Share your daily SOAK on **Facebook.com/GoodMorningGirlsWLW**

Instagram: WomenLivingWell #GoodMorningGirls

GMG Bible Coloring Chart

COLORS	KEYWORDS
PURPLE	God, Jesus, Holy Spirit, Saviour, Messiah
PINK	women of the Bible, family, marriage, parenting, friendship, relationships
RED	love, kindness, mercy, compassion, peace, grace
GREEN	faith, obedience, growth, fruit, salvation, fellowship, repentance
YELLOW	worship, prayer, praise, doctrine, angels, miracles, power of God, blessings
BLUE	wisdom, teaching, instruction, commands
ORANGE	prophecy, history, times, places, kings, genealogies, people, numbers, covenants, vows, visions, oaths, future
BROWN/GRAY	Satan, sin, death, hell, evil, idols, false teachers, hypocrisy, temptation

Introduction to the Book of Luke

The book of Luke is a vivid account of the life of Jesus. Luke takes us on an exciting journey from Jesus' birth, to Jesus' public ministry, to Jesus' death, resurrection and ascension into heaven. Salvation is clearly found in no one else but Jesus!

Luke was a doctor and he took special care to record everything accurately. Of all the gospels, Luke gives us the most detailed account of Jesus' birth. Luke shows the humanity of Jesus through showcasing his genealogy, his birth story, his growth as a boy, his prayer life and the betrayal and denial from some of his closest friends.

Jesus' many miracles and parables, written in this book, along with his compassion for the outcasts and sinners, and his love for women and children, draw us in deeper to understanding our Savior. The climax is when Jesus rises from the dead and ascends into heaven!

Luke not only penned this book but he also wrote the book of Acts. These two books combined, make up one-fourth of the New Testament!

Author: Luke the physician (the only Gentile author in the New Testament)

Date: 63 AD

Key Verse: *"For unto you is born this day in the city of David a Savior, who is Christ the Lord."* Luke 2:11

Outline:

1. **The introduction (1:1-4)**
2. **Jesus is born (1:5-2:52)**
3. **Jesus' preparation for public ministry (3:1-4:13)**
4. **Jesus' ministry in Galilee (4:14-9:50)**
5. **Jesus' journey to Jerusalem (9:51-19:27)**
6. **Jesus' teaching ministry in Jerusalem (19:28-21:38)**
7. **Jesus' death (22:1-23:56)**
8. **Jesus' resurrection (24:1-53)**

Major Themes:

Jesus' Humanity:

The book of Matthew shows Jesus as the King. The Book of Mark shows Jesus as a servant. The book of Luke shows Jesus as the Son of Man. His humanity is seen through his genealogy, birth account, his growth as a boy, his prayer life and his suffering.

Jesus' Teaching and Miracles:

Luke covers over 25 of Jesus' parables and 20 miracles.

Jesus' Compassion:

The book of Luke focuses more than any other gospel—on the poor, the outcasts, and sinners. He also showcases Jesus' concern for women and children. Luke emphasizes Jesus' mercy and compassion and warns against pride and self-righteousness.

Jesus' Prayer Life:

The book of Luke records more prayers of Jesus, than any other.

Salvation through Jesus:

Luke makes salvation clear to all who respond with repentance. It comes through the shed blood of the baby born in Bethlehem, who died on the cross and rose again three days later.

The Death and Resurrection of Jesus:

Luke gives the account of Jesus' death, resurrection and ascension. He continues the account of his ascension in his next book of the Bible, Acts.

Jesus came on a mission—to seek and to save the lost. I can't wait to take this journey with you, through the book of Luke, as we grow closer to our Savior.

Let's get started.

Keep walking with the King!

For nothing is impossible

with God.

Luke 1:37

Reflection Question:

The world says believe and you will receive. If you can dream it, you can achieve it. But that is not what Luke 1:37 says. It says nothing is impossible "with God." It is God who is the source of all power and possibilities.

Tell of a time, when you saw God do something impossible in your own life or the life of someone you know.

Luke 1

S—The S stands for *Scripture*

O—The O stands for *Observation*

A—The A stands for *Application*

K—The K stands for *Kneeling in Prayer*

For unto you is born this day in the city of David a Savior, who is Christ the Lord.

Luke 2:11

Reflection Question:

The King of Kings, the Messiah, Emmanuel—God with us, the Alpha and Omega, the beginning and the end, our glorious Savior was born! Oh what good news this is!!!

Have you placed your faith in Jesus for the forgiveness of your sins? If you haven't—do it today! If you have, share your testimony. When did Jesus become your personal savior?

Luke 2

S—The S stands for *Scripture*

O—The O stands for *Observation*

A—The A stands for *Application*

K—The K stands for *Kneeling in Prayer*

> When Jesus had been baptized and was praying,
> the heavens were opened, and the Holy Spirit descended
> on him in bodily form, like a dove;
> and a voice came from heaven,
> "You are my beloved Son; with you I am well pleased."
>
> Luke 3:21, 22

Reflection Question:

At Jesus' baptism, we see the trinity—God the Father, God the Son and God the Holy Spirit—3 in 1. It boggles my mind to try to grasp the awe of the trinity. I am so thankful that we will have trillions of years in heaven, to explore this mystery.

How does pondering, how awesome our triune God is, encourage you today?

Luke 3

S—The S stands for **Scripture**

O—The O stands for **Observation**

A—The A stands for **Application**

K—The K stands for **Kneeling in Prayer**

Jesus answered him, "It is written,

"'You shall worship the Lord your God,

and him only shall you serve.'"

Luke 4:8

Reflection Question:

When Jesus was tempted in the wilderness, he used scripture to fight temptation. He did not use his supernatural power but rather he fought by simply wielding the sword of God's Word.

When we are tempted, we have the same resource available to us that Jesus used—God's Word. In what areas of your life, do you need to be better armed with God's Word, to help you fight your temptations?

Luke 4

S—The S stands for *Scripture*

O—The O stands for *Observation*

A—The A stands for *Application*

K—The K stands for *Kneeling in Prayer*

Jesus answered, "Those who are well have no need of a physician, but those who are sick. I have not come to call the righteous but sinners to repentance."

Luke 5:31,32

Reflection Question:

Jesus came for those who were not just sick WITH sin but also sick OF their sin. He did not come for the self-righteous but for those who are humble enough to admit they are a sinner, in need of a savior.

Physicians fix broken bones and give healing to wounds. Jesus is the great Physician. What is one area where you need spiritual healing in your life or you have experienced his spiritual healing?

Luke 5

S—The S stands for *Scripture*

O—The O stands for *Observation*

A—The A stands for *Application*

K—The K stands for *Kneeling in Prayer*

> *Love your enemies,*
> *do good to those who hate you,*
> *bless those who curse you,*
> *pray for those who abuse you.*
>
> *Luke 6:27,28*

Reflection Question:

Jesus doesn't just tell us to love our enemies but he tells us how to do it. He tells us to do good to them, bless them and pray for them. We may not feel a warm feeling of love towards them, but there are no loopholes here. We are to love our enemies through visible actions.

Do you have an enemy? How can you show them love this week?

Luke 6

S—The S stands for *Scripture*

O—The O stands for *Observation*

A—The A stands for *Application*

K—The K stands for *Kneeling in Prayer*

I tell you, her sins,

which are many,

are forgiven for she loved much.

Luke 7:47

Reflection Question:

The woman, who washed Jesus' feet with her tears and hair, had sinned greatly in the past. But her humility and her deep emotional love for Jesus showed that she understood how great God's forgiveness is.

Pause for a moment and think back over your past and all of the sins you have committed in your lifetime.

Now take a moment and write a personal prayer of thanksgiving to Jesus, for his great love and forgiveness of your sins.

Luke 7

S—The S stands for *Scripture*

O—The O stands for *Observation*

A—The A stands for *Application*

K—The K stands for *Kneeling in Prayer*

Do not fear;
only believe.
Luke 8:50

Reflection Question:

When Jairus heard his daughter was dead, he may have lost hope. Perhaps he felt, God did not come through and he was too late. But God's timing is always right. He can make what is dead—come alive!

God was stretching Jairus' faith. All Jairus had to do was simply believe Jesus' words to be true.

Jesus said: "Do not fear only Believe." Is there an area in your life where fear has crept in and God is stretching your faith?

Luke 8

S—The S stands for *Scripture*

O—The O stands for *Observation*

A—The A stands for *Application*

K—The K stands for *Kneeling in Prayer*

Jesus said: "If anyone would come after me, let him deny himself and take up his cross daily and follow me."

Luke 9:23

Reflection Question:

Jesus told his disciples, if they were going to follow him, they were going to have to take up his cross daily. This was not easy to hear, for the disciples knew that the cross was the way to execute people.

The life of a Christian—is a life of self-denial, sacrifice and of dying to our own wants and desires…daily. In what area of your life has selfishness creeped in? How can you live a surrendered life daily?

Luke 9

S—The S stands for *Scripture*

O—The O stands for *Observation*

A—The A stands for *Application*

K—The K stands for *Kneeling in Prayer*

You shall love the Lord your God with all your heart and with all your soul and with all your strength and with all your mind, and love your neighbor as yourself.

Luke 10:27

Reflection Question:

There is a common mantra in our world that encourages us to love ourselves. Jesus knows the heart of man. We already naturally love ourselves and so we are commanded to love others LIKE we love ourselves.

Just like we care about our own concerns and interests, we should care about the concerns and interests of others. Who in your life needs more of your love and care today?

Luke 10

S—The S stands for *Scripture*

O—The O stands for *Observation*

A—The A stands for *Application*

K—The K stands for *Kneeling in Prayer*

Lord, teach us to pray.

Luke 11:1

Reflection Question:

Learning to pray is of utmost importance! Jesus did not teach his disciples how to preach, but he did teach them how to pray. The prayer in Luke 11, is not meant to be recited as a ritual, but rather as a pattern for our prayer life. After Jesus gave the pattern, he then gave an example of the boldness and persistence he wants us to have in our prayers.

Pause and pray through the Lord's Prayer today. Then consider, is there something you have given up praying for that you need to boldly and persistently begin praying for again? Write your prayer below.

Luke 11

S—The S stands for *Scripture*

O—The O stands for *Observation*

A—The A stands for *Application*

K—The K stands for *Kneeling in Prayer*

> *Be on your guard
> against all covetousness,
> for one's life does not consist
> in the abundance of his possessions.*
>
> *Luke 12:15*

Reflection Question:

The world system tells us that success and possessions deserve a high five, but at the end of the parable in Luke 12, God calls the rich man a fool! The only way to conquer a greedy heart is to believe that life does not consist in the abundance of our possessions.

Do you struggle with this? Jesus tells us to "be on guard." How can you guard and protect yourself from falling into the temptation of desiring an abundance of possessions?

Luke 12

S—The S stands for *Scripture*

O—The O stands for *Observation*

A—The A stands for *Application*

K—The K stands for *Kneeling in Prayer*

Behold, some are last who will be first,

and some are first who will be last.

Luke 13:30

Reflection Question:

To God, it does not matter what our standing in this world is. Money, titles, status, beauty, lineage and good works are not what God looks at. Salvation is based on Jesus' grace alone.

Do you, at times, feel jealous of others whose standing in this world is higher than yours? One of the great mysteries of the gospel is how those who are first in this world are last in the next. How does this truth bring you comfort today?

Luke 13

S—The S stands for **Scripture**

O—The O stands for **Observation**

A—The A stands for **Application**

K—The K stands for **Kneeling in Prayer**

For everyone who exalts himself will be humbled, and he who humbles himself will be exalted.

Luke 14:11

Reflection Question:

Jesus was the ultimate example of one who deserved the highest exaltation but he was humble. True humility does not have too high of an opinion of oneself and is others-centered rather than self-centered.

We are promised that those who humble themselves will one day—in eternity—be exalted. In what area of your life, do you need to work on humility?

Luke 14

S—The S stands for *Scripture*

O—The O stands for *Observation*

A—The A stands for *Application*

K—The K stands for *Kneeling in Prayer*

There is joy before the angels of God over one sinner who repents.

Luke 15:10

Reflection Question:

The parables in Luke 15, show us that God goes after the lost and heaven celebrates when they are found. Nothing is more precious to us as when it is lost. Think of your car keys—if they are lost—you search until they are found. And when they are found—you rejoice. In the same way, the angels rejoice when a sinner repents.

Who have you recently shared the love of Jesus or the gospel with? If you haven't had this opportunity, write a prayer for someone who is lost and ask God for boldness.

Luke 15

S—The S stands for **Scripture**

O—The O stands for **Observation**

A—The A stands for **Application**

K—The K stands for **Kneeling in Prayer**

You cannot serve God and money.

Luke 16:13

Reflection Question:

Many say that they love God but they spend their lives sacrificing to get more money. This is not about the size of our bank accounts but about the condition of our hearts. A poor greedy, jealous person may serve money more than a rich grateful, generous person. God knows the truth about our hearts by what we do with our money, in secret.

Are you tempted to serve money? In what ways and how do you overcome it?

Luke 16

S—The S stands for **Scripture**

O—The O stands for **Observation**

A—The A stands for **Application**

K—The K stands for **Kneeling in Prayer**

If you had faith like a grain of mustard seed,

you could say to this mulberry tree,

'Be uprooted and planted in the sea,'

and it would obey you.

Luke 17:6

Reflection Question:

Jesus tells the apostles, if they had faith the size of a mustard seed, they could uproot a mulberry tree. A mulberry tree has deep and strong roots and a mustard seed is tiny. Jesus says this right after telling the disciples to forgive offenses done to them. Many times, relational wounds run deep. Through faith—God can restore relationships. It's not about the size of our problem or our faith but the size of our great God.

In what area of your life, do you need to increase your faith today?

Luke 17

S—The S stands for **Scripture**

O—The O stands for **Observation**

A—The A stands for **Application**

K—The K stands for **Kneeling in Prayer**

> *Always pray and do not lose heart.*
> *Luke 18:1*

Reflection Question:

The persistent prayer of the widow is an example of how we must continue to pray and not give up. God does not delay in answering because he is waiting to be changed but because he is doing a changing work inside of us. God is good and he wants us to pray to him, day and night.

Are you discouraged in your prayer life right now? Have you given up or given only minimal time to prayer? There is power in prayer! What has God laid on your heart, that you should be praying more for?

Luke 18

S—The S stands for **Scripture**

O—The O stands for **Observation**

A—The A stands for **Application**

K—The K stands for **Kneeling in Prayer**

> *For the Son of Man came to seek and to save the lost.*
>
> *Luke 19:10*

Reflection Question:

Jesus came to seek and save the lost.
Jesus came to seek and to save you!
This is the heart of the gospel.

How long have you been saved? Never let the excitement of this truth and the passionate love God has for you, grow cold. Reflect on the fact that Jesus knows YOUR name. How does this make you feel?

Luke 19

S—The S stands for *Scripture*

O—The O stands for *Observation*

A—The A stands for *Application*

K—The K stands for *Kneeling in Prayer*

Render to Caesar the things that are Caesar's, and to God the things that are God's.

Luke 20:24

Reflection Question:

Everything belongs to God but Jesus recognized the authority of the government. When the government does not oppose God's commands, we are to obey.

We all have a dual citizenship. We are citizens of the country we live in and citizens of heaven. How does this truth make a difference in your life?

Luke 20

S—The S stands for *Scripture*

O—The O stands for *Observation*

A—The A stands for *Application*

K—The K stands for *Kneeling in Prayer*

Heaven and earth will pass away, but my words will not pass away.

Luke 21:33

Reflection Question:

Nothing in this world will last forever. We must not depend on the words we hear, the things we read or the possessions we own, to sustain us. It is God's Word that is powerful and eternal. His Words will last forever!

Do you find yourself tempted to substitute the words of this world for the Words of God? How can you make God's Word more of a priority in your life?

Luke 21

S—The S stands for *Scripture*

O—The O stands for *Observation*

A—The A stands for *Application*

K—The K stands for *Kneeling in Prayer*

> He took bread, and when he had given thanks,
> he broke it and gave it to them, saying,
> "This is my body, which is given for you.
> Do this in remembrance of me."
>
> Luke 22:19

Reflection Question:

Every time we wake up and forget to talk to Jesus—we have forgotten. Every time we give into temptation and sin—we have forgotten. Every time we become independent of God and live life on our own terms—we have forgotten. Taking communion helps us to remember. We remember Jesus' broken body and blood spilled out, for us.

Have you forgotten or grown numb to the truth of what Jesus did for you on the cross? Take some time right now and remember.

Luke 22

S—The S stands for *Scripture*

O—The O stands for *Observation*

A—The A stands for *Application*

K—The K stands for *Kneeling in Prayer*

And Jesus said, "Father, forgive them, for they know not what they do."

Luke 23:34

Reflection Question:

Jesus knew that those who crucified him were spiritually blind. They did not know what they were doing and he offered love to his enemies, just as he commands us to love our enemies.

Is there a spiritually blind person in your life, who has hurt you and who you need to forgive? This does not mean that you will be reconciled with them. For reconciliation, repentance is required. But forgiveness frees you from bitterness and resentment. Who do you need to forgive today?

Luke 23

S—The S stands for *Scripture*

O—The O stands for *Observation*

A—The A stands for *Application*

K—The K stands for *Kneeling in Prayer*

> *He is not here,*
> *but has risen.*
> *Luke 24:6*

Reflection Question:

Some of the most beautiful words in scripture are these: "He is not here, but has risen." This is what sets Jesus apart, from all other religions in history. You can search every grave but you will not find him there. Jesus lived a sinless life and death had no grip on him. Our God is alive!

Because Jesus is alive, our passions, our priorities, our plans and our past times should look different. How has Jesus changed your life?

Luke 24

S—The S stands for *Scripture*

O—The O stands for *Observation*

A—The A stands for *Application*

K—The K stands for *Kneeling in Prayer*

Made in the USA
Middletown, DE
30 November 2020